Lord, Make Haste to Help Me!

Also by Sarah Christmyer

Guided journals for Bible reading

- Create in me a Clean Heart: Ten Minutes a Day in the Penitential Psalms

- The Bible Timeline Guided Journal

Bible studies from *The Great Adventure* Catholic Bible Study Program (with Jeff Cavins):

- The Bible Timeline: The Story of Salvation

- Unlocking the Mystery of the Bible (previously A Quick Journey through the Bible)

- Matthew: the King and his Kingdom

- Acts: the Spread of the Kingdom

- James: Pearls for Wise Living

- Psalms: the School of Prayer (with Tim Gray)

- The Prophets: Messengers of God's Mercy (with Thomas Smith)

***Hearts Aflame* Bible studies (with Gayle Somers)**

- Genesis Part I: God and His Creation

- Genesis Part II: God and His Family

Books (contributing author)

- Walk in Her Sandals: Experiencing Christ's Passion through the Eyes of Women (Ed. Kelly Wahlquist)

LORD, Make Haste to Help Me!

Seven Psalms to Pray in Times of Need

SARAH CHRISTMYER

Unless otherwise stated, Scripture quotations are from The Catholic Edition of the Revised Standard Version of the Bible, copyright ©1965, 1966 by the Division of Christian Education of the National Council of the Churches of Christ in the United States of America. Used by permission. All rights reserved.

www.ComeIntotheWord.com

Cover by Cynthia Oswald
Photo © Sarah Christmyer
Interior design by Stella Ziegler

ISBN-10: 1540732320
ISBN-13: 978-1540732323

O God, make speed to save me:
*O L*ORD*, make haste to help me!*

*[This phrase] embraces all the feelings which can
be implanted in human nature, and can be fitly and
satisfactorily adapted to every condition, and all assaults.
Since it contains an invocation of God against every
danger, it contains humble and pious confession, it
contains the watchfulness of anxiety and continual fear,
it contains the thought of one's own weakness, confidence
in the answer, and the assurance of a present and ever
ready help. For one who is constantly calling on his
protector, is certain that He is always at hand. [...]*

*This verse, I say, will be found helpful and useful to
every one of us in whatever condition we may be.*

—John Cassian (c. 360–433)

"Lo, I am with you always."

—Jesus (Matthew 28:20)

Contents

Introduction

O God, come to my assistance;
O Lord, make haste to help me!

Who hasn't prayed this, or something like it, at some time in their life?

It comes from Psalm 70, where it is a strong call for rescue. But those words are far more than a cry for help. The early desert fathers repeated this verse throughout the day as a way to pray constantly. As a prayer, it expresses complete dependence on God and trust in his providence for our needs. No wonder these words are the starting point of prayer in the Liturgy of the Hours, whether they lead into praise or a prayer for help.[1] The phrase "O God, come to my assistance; O LORD, make haste to help me!" is a password of sorts, an "Open, Sesame!" that opens a door into the presence of God and places us at his feet.

---

1 *Every hour of prayer in the Divine Office begins with a call for the Lord's help, for without him we can do nothing—not even pray. Except for Morning Prayer, which begins with the invitatory "Lord, open our lips: and we shall praise your name," each hour begins with the opening verse of Psalm 70.*

As is typical of Hebrew poetry, this verse gives us one thought in two parallel ways in order to deepen its meaning. "God" in the first line is *Elohim* in Hebrew. It's the name used in Genesis 1:1 of the Creator and Lord of the universe. "God, come to my assistance" sounds formal: I need help, so I turn to someone powerful.

The second line gets more personal: "O LORD, make haste to help me!" Not only does the psalmist cry, "come quick!" as though he has a claim on God; he also calls him "LORD" — that is, YHWH or Yahweh — the personal name God revealed to Moses at the burning bush. It means, literally, "I AM." And as the LORD made clear to Moses, he is the God WHO IS close to his people. He is the one who sees their affliction, hears their cry, knows their suffering, and comes down to deliver them.[2]

> Whenever "Lord" in the Bible is in all capital letters, it translates the Hebrew *YHWH* (Yahweh). It means "I am" — it is the personal name of Israel's God.

The Psalms teach us to pray

Nearly half of the 150 Psalms can be classified as some sort of psalm of lament: an expression of sorrow or anguish accompanied by a plea for God's blessing or intervention. With few exceptions, those Psalms cry out specifically to YHWH. And running through them like a thread are cries of urgency like the one in Psalm 70. *Make haste! Hurry up! Come quick, do not delay!*

The Psalms are a school of prayer in which we can learn to gather our troubles, fears, inadequacies, and needs and take them to the One who loves us. With confidence, we can cry with the psalmist, "O LORD, make haste to help me!"

---

2   See Exodus 3, especially verse 7.

How we will do it

In the following pages, you will find reflections on seven psalms that give us a pattern for praying in times of need. In each one, the psalmist starts from a different place:

- In **Psalm 121**, a pilgrim seems to be answering a fellow traveler who's looking for help. In answer, he lifts his eyes to the hills and confidently proclaims his certainty that help comes from the Lord.

- **Psalm 13** is a classic lament psalm that teaches us how to turn our anguish to rejoicing by shifting our focus to God.

- In **Psalm 86**, the psalmist pours his distress out to God and begs for strength and comfort based on God's merciful love.

- The author of **Psalm 62** has been waiting and waiting … and is learning to rest in God and hope.

- **Psalm 46** proclaims God's strength and ever-present help even when the world seems to be falling apart.

- **Psalm 61** is a faint cry from a man who's been pursued to the ends of the earth, calling on God to restore him.

- And in closing, **Psalm 23** is not a cry for help at all but a statement of trust so strong that not even a walk through the valley of death will shake it. The spirit of Psalm 23 is our goal.

This journal is designed to help you get the most out of each psalm by reflecting on it for a short time every day for five days. Each day you will go a little bit deeper and allow the Word to make its way into your heart and speak to you.

There is room for you to write your observations and the fruits of your meditation and prayer. Journaling is an excellent way to reinforce what you hear and recall later what the Spirit brings to your mind. The more you allow the Word to penetrate your heart, and the more you allow it to work *in* you—the more it will transform your life.

What to expect

—*Monday: Prepare your heart*

The first day, you will read a reflection on that week's psalm before praying it out loud. The psalm is included at the start of the chapter but you may find it easier to keep your Bible beside you to refer to. As the week goes on you may find it helpful to highlight key words, things that stand out to you, parallels and patterns, and so on.

—*Tuesday – Friday: Prayerful reading*

Days 2-5 involve 10 minutes a day of prayerful meditation on the same psalm, going a little further each day in prayer. The steps are based on a time-tested method of reading Scripture so it becomes a prayerful conversation with the Lord. That method is called *lectio divina* — "spiritual reading," or, literally, "divine reading."

The process of *lectio divina* is simple:

- You read

- You prayerfully think about what you read

- You listen to the Word speak to your heart and then respond to God

- You rest in his presence

Each step of the way, you are guided so that your meditation is infused with prayer. You can spend 10-15 minutes a day, or you can spend longer—it's up to you. If you are not familiar with *lectio divina*, there is a brief guide in the next section. Additional prompts are provided in the first chapter, for Psalm 121, to get you started.

Ultimately, the word of God is not a book but a person who loves you and longs to connect with you on an intimate spiritual level. **Commit to offering up just 1% of your waking hours to get to know God.** Even 10-15 minutes a day will help you get away, open your heart, and hear his voice.

As you join me to *Come into the Word* over the next weeks, I pray you will discover the living Word of God within the written words of the Psalms. May you learn to call on him for help and experience his presence in a new way in your life.

For the glory of God,
Sarah Christmyer
December 2016
Philadelphia

Questions? Email me: sarah@ComeIntotheWord.com.

How to pray with Scripture: a brief guide to *lectio divina*

There is one particular way of listening to what the Lord wishes to tell us in his word and of letting ourselves be transformed by the Spirit. It is what we call lectio divina.

—*Pope Francis (Evangelii Gaudium, 152)*

rowing up in a Protestant family, I was used to settling down with my Bible and reading until I heard the Lord speaking to me. Little did I know, I was unconsciously following a very ancient practice of praying with Scripture. In the 11th century, a monk named Guigo the Carthusian described it as four rungs of a ladder that leads from earth to heaven: Reading, meditating, praying, and contemplating. The first step, reading (in Latin: *lectio*), gives the practice its name: *lectio divina*, divine (or spiritual) reading. When these steps are followed, the reader is drawn into a prayerful conversation with the Lord.

The "four Rs" of *lectio divina*

If you're new to *lectio divina*, it might be useful to think of these steps as four "Rs" that lead you into an intimate conversation with God: **Read — Reflect — Respond — Rest.**

It's not complicated.

You simply read and think carefully about what you read … listen for what God might be saying to you … talk to him about what you hear, resolving to follow what he tells you … and rest in his presence.

Here's how it's done:

1. Pray before you begin

> *Prayer should accompany the reading of Sacred Scripture, so that God and man may talk together; for "we speak to Him when we pray; we hear Him when we read the divine saying."*
>
> —*Pope Paul VI (Dei Verbum, 25)*

Open your heart and ask the Lord to speak. Prepare to listen. If you're distracted, ask for help: ask God to help you hear and focus. Ask Jesus, the living Word, to speak to you. Ask the Holy Spirit to come and fill you. Ask Mary, Mother of the Word, to pray for you. She more than any other human knows what it is like to receive God's word and ponder it in such a way that it bears fruit.

2. Read

> *[Lectio Divina] consists of reading God's word in a moment of prayer and allowing it to enlighten and renew us.*
>
> —*Pope Francis (Evangelii Gaudium, 152)*

Choose a small passage of Scripture. Read it slowly three to five times or more until you are very familiar with what is being said.

Explore the passage you are reading. Notice details, gather facts. Look for the Who, What, When, and Where. Pay attention to images, to patterns, to things that are repeated. It is most helpful to write down the things that you notice, or to underline and make notes on the text itself. The text of the Psalms is provided in this journal for that purpose.

3. Reflect

In the presence of God, during a recollected reading of the text, it is good to ask, for example: "Lord, what does this text say to me?

—Pope Francis (Evangelii Gaudium, 153)

Turn from thinking and observing to meditating. The idea behind meditating is to mentally "chew" on the Word of God, getting out every last bit of flavor.

How do you "chew" on the Word? Think. Ponder. Ask things like How? Why? What does it mean?

As you reflect, ask God to speak through his Word to you. Set aside things you don't understand for another day. Listen for God's still, small voice within your heart.

4. Respond

…no one is more patient than God our Father…. He simply asks that we sincerely look at our life and present ourselves honestly before him, and that we be willing to continue to grow, asking from him what we ourselves cannot as yet achieve.

—Pope Francis (Evangelii Gaudium, 153)

Talk to the Lord about what you hear. If you hear a question — answer. If you have a question — ask. If you feel grateful — give thanks. There's not one right way to talk to God. Here are some biblical examples:

- Mary pondered what she heard in her heart (Luke 2:19).

- Abraham argued with God (Genesis 18:16-33).

- Jacob wrestled with him (Genesis 32:22-32).

- The father of the son possessed by demons said: "Lord I believe; help my unbelief!" (Mark 9:23-24).

What is in your heart? Talk to God about it. Stay with Him and expect an answer. As you pray, listen. And resolve to act on what you hear.

5. Rest in God's presence and love.

> Lectio Divina *is truly 'capable of opening up to the faithful the treasures of God's word, but also of bringing about an encounter with Christ, the living word of God.'*
>
> —*Pope Benedict XVI (Verbum Domini, 87)*

Sometimes this step of resting is called "contemplation." It is less something you do than it is the result of what you have been doing. Your mind is lifted to God, and you experience His presence with joy and peace.

For more information about *lectio divina* and free downloads, including a one-page handout with a suggested journal format, go to the "Take it to" tab on my website: http://www.ComeIntotheWord.com.

Take it with you:
Planting the Word in your heart

I have laid up thy word in my heart,
that I might not sin against thee.

—*Psalm 119:11*

*W*hen God speaks to you, resolve to plant his Word in your heart where it can take root and transform you from the inside out.

You will be doing this as you ponder the Psalms in this journal. Another way is to memorize Scripture. It's easier than you might think. Choose a verse that speaks to you from the psalm you're reading, copy it onto a small card and carry it with you during the day. Take out the card whenever you have a few moments and repeat it to yourself (the reference too, so you know where to find it in your Bible!) until you know it. Or put a reminder on your smart phone. Set your alarm for noon and recite the verse before praying the Angelus. Do whatever will help you remember.

When you're done with one verse, post it over your desk or above your kitchen sink or on the dashboard of your car—somewhere you will see it and remember to review it. Meanwhile, start learning a new verse. Over time, you'll find that the Holy Spirit brings them to mind when you need them.

"I Lift Up My Eyes to the Hills"
Psalm 121

Assurance of God's Protection

Psalm 121

A Song of Ascents.

1   I lift up my eyes to the hills.
        From whence does my help come?
2   My help comes from the Lord,
        who made heaven and earth.
3   He will not let your foot be moved,
        he who keeps you will not slumber.
4   Behold, he who keeps Israel
        will neither slumber nor sleep.
5   The Lord is your keeper;
        the Lord is your shade
        on your right hand.

6   The sun shall not smite you by day,
      nor the moon by night.
7   The Lord will keep you from all evil;
      he will keep your life.
8   The Lord will keep
      your going out and your coming in
      from this time forth and for evermore.

MONDAY

Prepare Your Heart

To help prepare your heart, a brief reflection on the psalm is followed by a slow reading of it.

† Find a quiet place where you can read and pray
without distraction.

† Close your eyes and place yourself in God's presence.

† Read the following:

I hated walking home after Daylight Savings ended. I didn't live far from where I babysat, but the road wasn't lit. Not even seeing houses along the way—houses of people I knew, who were friendly—erased the nagging fear that something could happen, I could be hurt, and no one would hear me. I'd clutch my bag, walk tall, then sprint until I came into range of the light from our kitchen window.

I've always lived in safe places. There's not much reason for my fear. I can't help thinking how much worse it would be, if there were. The road traveled by pilgrims to Jerusalem in ancient times was known for its dangers. There were the physical dangers of heat and sunstroke; bandits hiding in wait by the road; superstitious fears of the moon … How did they do it?

"I lift my eyes to the hills," wrote the psalmist on his journey to the hills surrounding that holy city. "Where does my help come from?"

"My help comes from the LORD, who made heaven and earth."

Psalm 121 is a beautiful psalm, loved by many as the "travelers psalm." It's one of 15 "songs of ascent" (Psalms 120-134) sung by pilgrims on their way to Jerusalem to celebrate one of the three annual pilgrim feasts of Passover, Pentecost, and Tabernacles. But all of us can pray this psalm. We all are pilgrims en route to the eternal city, God's dwelling place. We all face danger on the way, and the answer to our cries for help is the same: "My help comes from the LORD."

Psalm 121 is short but it is rich with truths to ponder. Wherever you are in your personal journey, whatever dangers or weaknesses you face, you can turn there for comfort and strength.

† Pray Psalm 121 out loud, as follows.

O God, come to my assistance; O LORD, make haste to help me!
Prayerfully read the psalm.
Glory Be…

TUESDAY
Read

Today we begin in earnest on the first step of lectio divina, *"Read," in which you ask yourself: "What does it say?" Over the next days you will read Psalm 121 a number of times, allowing it to make a place your heart.*

† Find a quiet place where you can read and pray without distraction.

† Close your eyes and place yourself in God's presence.

† Pray:

Lord, inspire me to read your Scriptures and to meditate upon them day and night.... I know that understanding and good intentions are worthless, unless rooted in your graceful love. I ask that the words of Scripture may also be not just signs on a page, but channels of grace into my heart.

—Origen of Alexandria

† Read Psalm 121 all the way through several times.

What stands out to you in this psalm? Are there any words or phrases that catch your eye? For example:

• What kinds of trials are named or alluded to? What do you notice about them?

• This psalm is personal. Notice all the times it says "my" and "you" and "your." My what? You(r) what? Make a list. Or—

• Notice how often the word "keep" is used. The repetition should draw your eye — it's done for emphasis, like we would underline or put something in bold. The Hebrew root is *smr*: "to keep, preserve, protect." "Keeper" is more properly "watchman" (as in our phrase, night watchman). Look closely at each instance of "keep." What do you learn?

Other things may stand out to you as well. There's no right or wrong thing to notice. Record your thoughts below.

_____

_____

_____

_____

_____

_____

_____

_____

_____

_____

† Pray Psalm 121 out loud, as follows.

O God, come to my assistance; O LORD, make haste to help me!
Prayerfully read the psalm.
Glory Be...

TAKE IT WITH YOU:

Copy the part of Psalm 121 that spoke most to you onto a small card or make a note on your smart phone. Carry it with you and meditate on it throughout the week. Repeat it until you know it by heart.

WEDNESDAY
Reflect

On the third day we reflect further on the psalm, returning to things noticed previously and moving from "what does it say?" to "what does it mean?" and "what does it mean to me?"

† Find a quiet place where you can read and pray
without distraction.

† Close your eyes and place yourself in God's presence.

† Pray:

Lord, inspire me to read your Scriptures and to meditate upon them day and night…. I know that understanding and good intentions are worthless, unless rooted in your graceful love. I ask that the words of Scripture may also be not just signs on a page, but channels of grace into my heart.

—*Origen of Alexandria*

Reflect on Psalm 121, recalling your previous observations. What else do you notice? Continue to read, lingering where your heart draws you. What do you hear God saying to you, personally? Write down in your journal the things that come to mind.

† Pray Psalm 121 out loud, as follows.

O God, come to my assistance; O LORD, *make haste to help me!*

Prayerfully read the psalm.

Glory Be…

✐ THURSDAY ✐
Respond

God's word does more than reveal truth. He speaks to us, personally, through the inspired words of the Bible. Today you will read Psalm 121 again, prayerfully, listening for his voice and responding to what you hear.

† Find a quiet place where you can read and pray
  without distraction.

† Close your eyes and place yourself in God's presence.

† Pray:

Lord, inspire me to read your Scriptures and to meditate upon them day and night.... I know that understanding and good intentions are worthless, unless rooted in your graceful love. I ask that the words of Scripture may also be not just signs on a page, but channels of grace into my heart.

—*Origen of Alexandria*

† Read Psalm 121 and recall what you have been hearing God
  say to your heart.

✐ **What is your response?** Talk to the Lord about it. Are you on a dangerous road? Are you exposed in some way? Is a friend in need of help, who you should pray for? How does this psalm speak to you? Tell the Lord what is in your heart. Record your response below.

† Pray Psalm 121 out loud, as follows.

O God, come to my assistance; O LORD, make haste to help me!

Prayerfully read the psalm.

Glory Be…

FRIDAY
Rest

The week of meditation ends with resting in God's love.

  † Find a quiet place where you can read and pray
    without distraction.

  † Close your eyes and place yourself in God's presence. Pray
    Psalm 121 out loud, as follows.

    O God, come to my assistance; O LORD, make haste to help me!

    Prayerfully read the psalm, recalling the things God has brought
    to your mind.

    Glory Be…

Fix your gaze upon God and rest in his merciful love.
Allow yourself to be quiet in his presence. Rest as though you are
lying in his arms. Let him fill you with comfort and peace.

Our Father…

I sought the Lord, and he answered me,
and delivered me from all my fears.

--Psalm 34:4

"How long, O Lord, how long?
Psalm 13

Prayer for deliverance from enemies

Psalm 13

To the choirmaster. A Psalm of David.

1   How long, O Lord? Wilt thou forget me for ever?
        How long wilt thou hide thy face from me?

2   How long must I bear pain[1] in my soul,
        and have sorrow in my heart all the day?
        How long shall my enemy be exalted over me?

3   Consider and answer me, O Lord my God;
        lighten my eyes, lest I sleep the sleep of death;

4   lest my enemy say, "I have prevailed over him";
        lest my foes rejoice because I am shaken.

---

1   Syr: Heb *hold counsels*

5   But I have trusted in thy steadfast love;
        my heart shall rejoice in thy salvation.
6   I will sing to the Lord,
        because he has dealt bountifully with me.

MONDAY
Prepare Your Heart

† Find a quiet place where you can read and pray
without distraction.

† Close your eyes and place yourself in God's presence.

† Read the following:

I remember the day it all got to be too much for me. Our
house had finally sold after two years sitting empty, but that hardly
made a difference. We sold at a loss, and my husband had been
without work for months. There was no money in the bank. We
had a toddler and a baby to care for, my grandfather had just died,
and we had just learned my mother had cancer. There was no
more space in me for worry and it all came spilling out.

"God!" I cried out from the floor, where I lay curled up in my grief.
"Where are you? Why don't you answer our prayers?!"

It all comes back as I read the beginning of Psalm 13:

> *How long, LORD? Will you utterly forget me?*
> *How long will you hide your face from me?*
> *How long must I carry sorrow in my soul,*
> *grief in my heart day after day?*
> *How long will my enemy triumph over me?*

How long … how long … how long … how long? Repetition strings out the anguish of the psalmist, helps you feel what he feels. *God, where are you when I need you? How long will this go on?*

Psalm 13 is what biblical scholars call an "individual lament": a psalm in which a person cries out to the LORD in time of personal need. There are more Psalms of individual lament in the Psalter than there are of any other type. Most of them follow the pattern we see here in Psalm 13: a cry of complaint or grievance; a plea for help; and an expression of trust and praise. The beauty of this pattern is that when we pray one of these Psalms from the heart, entering personally into its opening plea, as we continue to read it takes our eyes off of the problem and directs them to God and his mercy. It actually lifts our hearts and teaches us to trust.

The psalmist continues: *Look at me! Answer me!* He's demanding, persistent. Some people think we shouldn't bother God with our personal troubles, that he has too many more important things on his mind, but the Psalms teach us otherwise. "My God!" he calls the LORD. *My* God. God deliberately established a personal relationship with his people. The psalmist claims God's attention based on that relationship, and so can we. The psalmist fears death; his enemies are getting the upper hand; and if he stumbles they will rejoice. All of these things deserve God's attention, and he knows it.

"But I trust in your mercy," he continues. The Grail translation begins, "As for me…."

"*But.*" "*As for me.*" This is a turning point, an about-face. Regardless of the situation and how it appears, the psalmist has come to a decision. He will trust in God's merciful love.

"Grant my heart joy in your salvation," the psalmist asks. He knows God is merciful, he knows God has saved and will save him again. God has blessed him and will bless again. The psalmist doesn't feel it, though, and he asks God to grant him joy in that knowledge. "I *will* sing to the LORD," he concludes. A determination to trust has risen from within, from the place where before there was only anxiety.

God's merciful love has upheld my husband and me through many difficult times, for nearly 30 years. Each incident helps me remember: God "has dealt bountifully with me!" When new trials come and I find myself crying out again, *God, where are you? How long before you answer?!* I turn to Psalms like this one. Pondering Psalm 13, I feel my heart turn and from it comes a determined cry: "As for me, I trust in your mercy."

"Mercy" here is *hesed* in Hebrew. You'll find this word all through the Psalms. Sometimes it's translated "steadfast love" or "loving-kindness," "loyalty," or even "grace."

It refers to the profound goodness and faithful love that God shows and has always shown his people just because they are his — because of their covenant relationship that makes them his beloved children and spouse.

As you meditate on Psalm 13 this week, you might want to remember that these are not just the words of the psalmist; they are words of the Lord as well. We can pray the first two sets of verses hearing Jesus on the Cross — and with him and the knowledge of God's saving victory, move to praise.

† Pray Psalm 13 out loud, as follows.

O God, come to my assistance; O LORD, *make haste to help me!*

Prayerfully read the psalm.

Glory Be...

TUESDAY
Read

† Find a quiet place where you can read and pray
without distraction.

† Close your eyes and place yourself in God's presence.

† Pray:

*Lord, inspire me to read your Scriptures and to meditate upon them day
and night.... I know that understanding and good intentions are worthless,
unless rooted in your graceful love. I ask that the words of Scripture may
also be not just signs on a page, but channels of grace into my heart.*

—*Origen of Alexandria*

† Read Psalm 13 all the way through several times.

What stands out to you in this psalm? Are there any
words or phrases that catch your eye? What do you notice about
them? Record your thoughts here or in a journal if desired:

---

† Pray Psalm 13 out loud, as follows.

O God, come to my assistance; O LORD, make haste to help me!
Prayerfully read the psalm.
Glory Be…

TAKE IT WITH YOU:

Copy the part of Psalm 13 that spoke most to you onto a small card or make a note on your smart phone. Carry it with you and meditate on it throughout the week. Repeat it until you know it by heart.

WEDNESDAY
Reflect

† Find a quiet place where you can read and pray
   without distraction.

† Close your eyes and place yourself in God's presence.

† Pray:

*Lord, inspire me to read your Scriptures and to meditate upon them day
and night.... I know that understanding and good intentions are worthless,
unless rooted in your graceful love. I ask that the words of Scripture may
also be not just signs on a page, but channels of grace into my heart.*

—*Origen of Alexandria*

Reflect on Psalm 13, recalling your previous observations.

Continue to read, lingering where your heart draws you. What
do you hear God saying to you, personally? Write down in your
journal the things that come to mind.

---

† Pray Psalm 13 out loud, as follows.

O God, come to my assistance; O LORD, make haste to help me!

Prayerfully read the psalm.

Glory Be…

⚮ THURSDAY ⚭
Respond

† Find a quiet place where you can read and pray
without distraction.

† Close your eyes and place yourself in God's presence.

† Pray:

*Lord, inspire me to read your Scriptures and to meditate upon them day
and night.... I know that understanding and good intentions are worthless,
unless rooted in your graceful love. I ask that the words of Scripture may
also be not just signs on a page, but channels of grace into my heart.*

—*Origen of Alexandria*

† Read Psalm 13 and recall what you have been hearing God
say to your heart.

❧ **What is your response?** Talk to him about it. Are you
wondering how long it will be before God answers the cry of your
heart? The more times you read Psalm 13, the deeper it will reach
into your soul. Pray with it again and tell him what is in your heart.
Record your response below:

_____

_____

_____

_____

† Pray Psalm 13 out loud, as follows.

O God, come to my assistance; O LORD, make haste to help me!

Prayerfully read the psalm.

Glory Be…

FRIDAY
Rest

† Find a quiet place where you can read and pray
without distraction.

† Close your eyes and place yourself in God's presence. Pray
Psalm 13 out loud, as follows.

O God, come to my assistance; O LORD, make haste to help me!

Prayerfully read the psalm, recalling the things God has brought
to your mind.

Glory Be...

Fix your gaze upon God and rest in his merciful love.
Allow yourself to be quiet in his presence. Rest as though you are
lying in his arms. Let him fill you with comfort and peace.

Our Father...

For thus said the Lord God, the Holy One of Israel,
"In returning and rest you shall be saved;
in quietness and in trust shall be your strength."

—Isaiah 30:15

"Give Ear, O Lord, to My Prayer"
Psalm 86

Supplication for Help Against Enemies

Psalm 86

A Prayer of David.

1   Incline thy ear, O Lord, and answer me,
        for I am poor and needy.
2   Preserve my life, for I am godly;
        save thy servant who trusts in thee.
        Thou art my God;
3   be gracious to me, O Lord,
        for to thee do I cry all the day.
4   Gladden the soul of thy servant,
        for to thee, O Lord, do I lift up my soul.
5   For thou, O Lord, art good and forgiving,
        abounding in steadfast love to all who call on thee.
6   Give ear, O Lord, to my prayer;

      hearken to my cry of supplication.

7 In the day of my trouble I call on thee,
      for thou dost answer me.

8 There is none like thee among the gods, O Lord,
      nor are there any works like thine.

9 All the nations thou hast made shall come
      and bow down before thee, O Lord,
      and shall glorify thy name.

10 For thou art great and doest wondrous things,
      thou alone art God.

11 Teach me thy way, O Lord,
      that I may walk in thy truth;
      unite my heart to fear thy name.

12 I give thanks to thee, O Lord my God, with my whole heart,
      and I will glorify thy name for ever.

13 For great is thy steadfast love toward me;
      thou hast delivered my soul from the depths of Sheol.

14 O God, insolent men have risen up against me;
      a band of ruthless men seek my life,
      and they do not set thee before them.

15 But thou, O Lord, art a God merciful and gracious,
      slow to anger and abounding in steadfast love
      and faithfulness.

16 Turn to me and take pity on me;
      give thy strength to thy servant,
      and save the son of thy handmaid.

17 Show me a sign of thy favor,
      that those who hate me may see and be put to shame
      because thou, Lord, hast helped me and comforted me.

MONDAY
Prepare Your Heart

† Find a quiet place where you can read and pray
without distraction.

† Close your eyes and place yourself in God's presence.

† Read the following:

I always think of what to say after the conversation is over. For an hour I sat and listened to my friend complain. The world is falling apart, she fears. "And can you believe those people who pray about every little problem — do they think God cares about a parking space?!" She was incensed. "God has way too much on his mind to worry about us and our lives," she said. "Global warming, world hunger, preserving marriage ... those are things I pray for."

I sat there sad and wondering, trying to figure out just who or what is her "God." Because the God I know is concerned with global issues *and* with the everyday things of life. He's personal. He loves me (and her and you and the person who prays for parking spaces). *Really* loves us. After my friend left, it dawned on me: "God" to her is an impersonal force. A distant power that should be bringing about peace and justice but that has fallen down on the job. Maybe, just maybe, this force will take notice if we pray. If the need is great enough. If we yell loud enough. But in the end, change is up to us.

How very different that is from the view of the believing Christian or Jew. Just look at Psalm 86:

This is a lament psalm, and it begins and ends with a plea for help. But it is suffused with trust in a God the psalmist *knows* will help him. "On the day of my distress I call to you," he says in verse 7, "for *you will answer* me."

The reason for his certainty lies smack in the center of the psalm (read verses 8-10). "Wondrous deeds" covers everything from creating the universe to intervening in the affairs of nations — the global issues my friend was concerned with. But God is more than a great and powerful force. The rest of the psalm highlights God's mercy. That is the *nature* of God, the thing that makes him stoop in his power and concern himself with our cries.

There's a lot to ponder in this psalm, but let's look at what it tells us about God.

Three times Psalms 86 speaks of the "name" of God (9,11,12). That is, his character. What you call a person helps define them. And in these 17 short verses, the psalmist names God 19 times. He also addresses him directly (calling him "you") or describes him ("your" ear, works, way, truth, etc.) more than 20 times. The psalmist may be in trouble, but his entire attention is on God to whom he speaks.

When you are meditating on Psalm 86, here are some things you might look for:

- Three names are used for God: LORD (*YHWH*, the intimate family name God gave Israel when he made them his people); Lord (*Adonai*, "my sovereign"); and God (*Elohim*, God. But note also "my God," which lays claim to their covenant relationship). What comes across with those different names?

- How is God described?

- Notice all the times "for" is used. That means "because." What reasons does the psalmist give, for God to answer and help him?

Perhaps it is because I am thinking of my friend, but I am most struck by how close the psalmist is to the Lord. The love in their relationship goes both ways! God may be the Great and Only, but that greatness is exercised on behalf of those he loves. The psalmist turns to him with as much confidence as a child turns to a beloved parent. He knows he can trust in his loving care.

† Pray Psalm 86 out loud, as follows.

O God, come to my assistance; O LORD, make haste to help me!

Prayerfully read the psalm.

Glory Be…

∾ TUESDAY ∾
Read

† Find a quiet place where you can read and pray
without distraction.

† Close your eyes and place yourself in God's presence.

† Pray:

*Lord, inspire me to read your Scriptures and to meditate upon them day
and night.... I know that understanding and good intentions are worthless,
unless rooted in your graceful love. I ask that the words of Scripture may
also be not just signs on a page, but channels of grace into my heart.*

——*Origen of Alexandria*

† Read Psalm 86 all the way through several times.

🦢 **What stands out to you in this psalm?** Are there any
words or phrases that catch your eye? What do you notice about
them? Record your thoughts.

_____

_____

_____

_____

_____

_____

_____

_____

_____

_____

_____

_____

_____

_____

_____

_____

_____

_____

_____

_____

_____

_____

† Pray Psalm 86 out loud, as follows.

O God, come to my assistance; O LORD, make haste to help me!

Prayerfully read the psalm.

Glory Be…

TAKE IT WITH YOU:

Copy the part of Psalm 86 that spoke most to you onto a small card or make a note on your smart phone. Carry it with you and meditate on it throughout the week. Repeat it until you know it by heart.

WEDNESDAY
Reflect

† Find a quiet place where you can read and pray
without distraction.

† Close your eyes and place yourself in God's presence.

† Pray:

*Lord, inspire me to read your Scriptures and to meditate upon them day
and night…. I know that understanding and good intentions are worthless,
unless rooted in your graceful love. I ask that the words of Scripture may
also be not just signs on a page, but channels of grace into my heart.*

—*Origen of Alexandria*

Reflect on Psalm 86, recalling your previous observations.

Continue to read, lingering where your heart draws you. What
do you hear God saying to you, personally? Write down in your
journal the things that come to mind.

_____

_____

_____

_____

_____

_____

_____

_____

_____

_____

_____

_____

_____

_____

_____

_____

_____

† Pray Psalm 86 out loud, as follows.

O God, come to my assistance; O LORD, make haste to help me!

Prayerfully read the psalm.

Glory Be…

⎰⎱ THURSDAY ⎰⎱
Respond

† Find a quiet place where you can read and pray
without distraction.

† Close your eyes and place yourself in God's presence.

† Pray:

*Lord, inspire me to read your Scriptures and to meditate upon them day
and night.... I know that understanding and good intentions are worthless,
unless rooted in your graceful love. I ask that the words of Scripture may
also be not just signs on a page, but channels of grace into my heart.*

—*Origen of Alexandria*

† Read Psalm 86 and recall what you have been hearing God
say to your heart.

What is your response? Tell God what is in your heart.
Record your response below.

_____

_____

_____

_____

_____

_____

_____

_____

_____

_____

_____

_____

_____

_____

_____

_____

_____

_____

_____

_____

_____

_____

† Pray Psalm 86 out loud, as follows.

O God, come to my assistance; O LORD, make haste to help me!

Prayerfully read the psalm.

Glory Be…

✐ FRIDAY ✐
Rest

† Find a quiet place where you can read and pray
without distraction.

† Close your eyes and place yourself in God's presence. Pray
Psalm 86 out loud, as follows.

O God, come to my assistance; O LORD, make haste to help me!

Prayerfully read the psalm, recalling the things God has brought
to your mind.

Glory Be…

🖎 **Fix your gaze upon God and rest in his merciful love**.
Allow yourself to be quiet in his presence. Rest as though you are
lying in his arms. Let him fill you with comfort and peace.

Our Father…

May you be strengthened with all power, according to his
glorious might, for all endurance and patience with joy, giving
thanks to the Father…. He has delivered us from the dominion
of darkness and transferred us to the kingdom of his beloved
Son, in whom we have redemption, the forgiveness of sins.

——*Colossians 1:11-14*

"For God Alone
My Soul Waits in Silence"
Psalm 62

Song of Trust in God Alone

Psalm 62

To the choirmaster: according to Jeduthun. A Psalm of David.

1   For God alone my soul waits in silence;
       from him comes my salvation.
2   He only is my rock and my salvation,
       my fortress; I shall not be greatly moved.
3   How long will you set upon a man
       to shatter him, all of you,
       like a leaning wall, a tottering fence?
4   They only plan to thrust him down from his eminence.
       They take pleasure in falsehood.

They bless with their mouths,
but inwardly they curse. *Selah*

5   For God alone my soul waits in silence,
for my hope is from him.

6   He only is my rock and my salvation,
my fortress; I shall not be shaken.

7   On God rests my deliverance and my honor;
my mighty rock, my refuge is God.

8   Trust in him at all times, O people;
pour out your heart before him;
God is a refuge for us. *Selah*

9   Men of low estate are but a breath,
men of high estate are a delusion;
in the balances they go up;
they are together lighter than a breath.

10   Put no confidence in extortion,
set no vain hopes on robbery;
if riches increase, set not your heart on them.

11   Once God has spoken;
twice have I heard this:
that power belongs to God;

12   and that to thee, O Lord, belongs steadfast love.
For thou dost requite a man
according to his work.

⟿ MONDAY ⟾
Prepare Your Heart

† Find a quiet place where you can read and pray
without distraction.

† Close your eyes and place yourself in God's presence.

† Read the following:

🕭 **Before our daughter could walk,** I would set her on the
floor on a blanket with a few toys while I did the dishes or dusted
or opened the mail. She always played happily by herself – as long
as I stayed within sight. If I stepped into the next room for even a
minute: "Waaaaaaah!" She cried like she'd been abandoned.

The children of Israel acted like that when God freed them from
Egypt. Like babies, they felt safe only when God was in plain
sight (or at least was immediately evident in smoke and fire or the
provision of water or food). The second they were in need, they
panicked and started to grumble and fear. "Waaaaaah…..!" they
cried. They forgot God's power and care and assumed they had
been abandoned.

"Look!" I want to shout at them. "Can't you see his love? Just
wait and he will come through!" But I have an advantage, reading
about Israel in the desert. I have the whole story spread out before
me and they are stuck in the beginning.

If only it was easy to step back and get that "eternal perspective" on my own life! Because even having known the power of God and his loving, caring presence in my life, there are times when I find myself stuck at this point in my story. My eyes turn from God and look at my situation, or they strain to penetrate the future, and I stumble. Like the children of Israel, I think God has gone away and I grumble and wail. Like my infant daughter, I think I have been abandoned.

"Lord, make haste to help me!" I cry. And sometimes his answer is, simply, *Wait. I'm here, though you can't see me. Trust in my love for you.*

When I can't find it in me to do that, Psalm 62 is a great help. It doesn't just tell me to wait, or even tell me how to wait. It *helps* me wait when I meditate on it and allow the Holy Spirit to pray it in me and through me.

It starts like this:

For God alone my soul waits in silence;
  from him comes my salvation.
He only is my rock and my salvation,
  my fortress; I shall not be greatly moved. (vss. 1-2)

The psalmist knows this in his head but it's as though he's trying to convince his heart. Very real enemies are after him and he's starting to feel "like a leaning wall, a tottering fence" (vs. 3). "How long" will you continue? He cries. Must he wait forever?

"For God alone my soul waits in silence," he repeats in verse 5. Only this time, with a difference that doesn't come across in this translation. In Hebrew, it's a command:

For God alone, my soul, wait in silence! For my hope is from him.

The general idea in verse 1 that salvation comes from God becomes the psalmist's personal hope. He grabs onto that hope and tells his soul to wait, to be silent – to rest in the knowledge of who God is and what that means for him. As his soul settles in confidence, he can declare:

He only is my rock and my salvation,
*   my fortress; I shall not be shaken.*
On God rests my deliverance and my honor;
*   my mighty rock, my refuge is God.* (vss. 6-7)

Let these verses soak into your heart and feel how your soul starts to move in sync with the psalmist's. His soul has moved into God's mighty fortress and now he calls out to the rest of us:

Trust in him at all times, O people;
*   pour out your heart before him;*
*   God is a refuge for us. Selah*

[...] power belongs to God;
*   ... to thee, O Lord, belongs steadfast love.* (vss. 8, 11-12)

God loves you! He loves you more than I love my daughter, more than you love those you watch over and care for. The wise parent knows when leaving a child alone for a time builds strength and confidence and faith and character ... and when it's time to step in and help. My visible absence didn't mean my eye wasn't on my little girl or that my ear didn't hear or that I wasn't ready to help. God isn't just loving, he IS love. In his very being, he is faithful, steadfast, merciful love. "Pour out your heart before him" and wait in silent peace.

† Pray Psalm 62 out loud, as follows.

O God, come to my assistance; O LORD, make haste to help me!

Prayerfully read the psalm.

Glory Be…

⤳ TUESDAY ⤳
Read

† Find a quiet place where you can read and pray
without distraction.

† Close your eyes and place yourself in God's presence.

† Pray:

*Lord, inspire me to read your Scriptures and to meditate upon them day
and night.... I know that understanding and good intentions are worthless,
unless rooted in your graceful love. I ask that the words of Scripture may
also be not just signs on a page, but channels of grace into my heart.*

——*Origen of Alexandria*

† Read Psalm 62 all the way through several times.

🍂 **What stands out to you in this psalm?** Are there any
words or phrases that catch your eye? What do you notice about
them? Record your thoughts.

_____

_____

_____

_____

_____

_____

_____

† Pray Psalm 62 out loud, as follows.

O God, come to my assistance; O Lord, make haste to help me!

Prayerfully read the psalm.

Glory Be…

TAKE IT WITH YOU:

Copy the part of Psalm 62 that spoke most to you onto a small card or make a note on your smart phone. Carry it with you and meditate on it throughout the week. Repeat it until you know it by heart.

WEDNESDAY
Reflect

† Find a quiet place where you can read and pray
without distraction.

† Close your eyes and place yourself in God's presence.

† Pray:

*Lord, inspire me to read your Scriptures and to meditate upon them day
and night.... I know that understanding and good intentions are worthless,
unless rooted in your graceful love. I ask that the words of Scripture may
also be not just signs on a page, but channels of grace into my heart.*

—*Origen of Alexandria*

Reflect on Psalm 62, recalling your previous observations.

Continue to read, lingering where your heart draws you. What
do you hear God saying to you, personally? Write down in your
journal the things that come to mind.

† Pray Psalm 62 out loud, as follows.

O God, come to my assistance; O LORD, make haste to help me!

Prayerfully read the psalm.

Glory Be…

☙ THURSDAY ❧
Respond

† Find a quiet place where you can read and pray
  without distraction.

† Close your eyes and place yourself in God's presence.

† Pray:

*Lord, inspire me to read your Scriptures and to meditate upon them day
and night.... I know that understanding and good intentions are worthless,
unless rooted in your graceful love. I ask that the words of Scripture may
also be not just signs on a page, but channels of grace into my heart.*

—*Origen of Alexandria*

† Read Psalm 62 and recall what you have been hearing God
  say to your heart.

What is your response? Talk to him about it. Record your
response below.

_____

_____

_____

_____

_____

_____

_____

† Pray Psalm 62 out loud, as follows.

O God, come to my assistance; O Lord, *make haste to help me!*

Prayerfully read the psalm.

Glory Be…

FRIDAY
Rest

† Find a quiet place where you can read and pray
without distraction.

† Close your eyes and place yourself in God's presence. Pray
Psalm 62 out loud, as follows.

O God, come to my assistance; O LORD, make haste to help me!

Prayerfully read the psalm, recalling the things God has brought
to your mind.

Glory Be…

Fix your gaze upon God and rest in his merciful love.
Allow yourself to be quiet in his presence. Rest as though you are
lying in his arms. Let him fill you with comfort and peace.

Our Father…

*Without having seen him you love him; though
you do not now see him you believe in him and
rejoice with unutterable and exalted joy.*

——1 Peter 1:8-9

"Be Still and Know that I am God"
Psalm 46

God's Defense of His City and People

Psalm 46

To the choirmaster. A Psalm of the Sons of Korah. According to Alamoth. A Song.

1   God is our refuge and strength,
        a very present help[1] in trouble.
2   Therefore we will not fear though the earth should change,
        though the mountains shake in the heart of the sea;
3   though its waters roar and foam,
        though the mountains tremble with its tumult. *Selah*
4   There is a river whose streams make glad the city of God,
        the holy habitation of the Most High.

---

1   Psalm 46:1 Or *well proved*

5   God is in the midst of her, she shall not be moved;
    God will help her right early.

6   The nations rage, the kingdoms totter;
    he utters his voice, the earth melts.

7   The Lord of hosts is with us;
    the God of Jacob is our refuge[2]. *Selah*

8   Come, behold the works of the Lord,
    how he has wrought desolations in the earth.

9   He makes wars cease to the end of the earth;
    he breaks the bow, and shatters the spear,
    he burns the chariots with fire!

10 "Be still, and know that I am God.
    I am exalted among the nations,
    I am exalted in the earth!"

11 The Lord of hosts is with us;
    the God of Jacob is our refuge[3]. *Selah*

---

2   Psalm 46:7 Or *fortress*
3   Psalm 46:11 Or *fortress*

✐◠ MONDAY ◠✐
Prepare Your Heart

† Find a quiet place where you can read and pray without distraction.

† Close your eyes and place yourself in God's presence.

† Read the following:

🍃**I was at the home of a friend** when the winds came, bending trees low to the ground and howling through the cracks, shaking the old house to its foundation. A large branch hit the house with a thud. A vase fell to the floor. My friend and I ran for the basement. Refuge!

I have seldom needed a real refuge in my life, having lived in times of peace and places of security. So when I read, in Psalm 46, "God is our refuge," to personalize it I usually think of physical storms. Today, as random violent acts increase in our cities and people like me are targeted for their beliefs and political parties swing to the edges, I begin to feel the need for refuge in a different way, and make the connection: Hate-filled mobs are like a storm you can't get away from. The earth feels like it is shifting beneath me, like it does with an earthquake.

The people who wrote the Bible were subject to both kinds of disaster. Refuge was needed from natural storms and men alike. Their lives were intimately connected to the earth and they used the language of the earth—mountains shaking, seas roaring, stars falling—to describe the impact of civil unrest and political upheaval.

Because they wrote the way they did (not just of disaster but of the help they found in God), we can go from the morning news to the refuge of the Bible. Psalm 46:1-2—

God is our refuge and strength,
>*a very present help in trouble.*
Therefore we will not fear though the earth should change,
>*though the mountains shake in the heart of the sea.*

Our world is changing, but God is still with us. "Very present" here is sometimes translated "ever-present" or "well-proved." His help is not only available when and where we need it; it's been tested and proved reliable. God does not change or "shake." We can trust him and not fear because he is solid when everything around us fails.

The psalm goes on to describe Jerusalem, the city where God chose to dwell. It is a picture of the Church. It cannot fall like the earth and nations can fall, because God who does not change lives within her:

God is in the midst of her, she shall not be moved;
>*God will help her right early.*
The nations rage, the kingdoms totter;
>*he utters his voice, the earth melts.*
The Lord of hosts is with us;
>*the God of Jacob is our refuge.* (vss. 5-7)

"Lord of hosts" is a particularly good name to use here for God. It refers to God as the lord or commander of the armies of heaven. Sometimes it's translated "God Almighty." He is with us in power!

Praying with this psalm as it calls me to think about who God is and what he has done has the effect of drawing me into God's strong arms. He provides a safe refuge regardless of the storm outside.

† Pray Psalm 46 out loud, as follows.

O God, come to my assistance; O Lord, make haste to help me!

Prayerfully read the psalm.

Glory Be...

✐ TUESDAY ✐
Read

† Find a quiet place where you can read and pray without distraction.

† Close your eyes and place yourself in God's presence.

† Pray:

Lord, inspire me to read your Scriptures and to meditate upon them day and night…. I know that understanding and good intentions are worthless, unless rooted in your graceful love. I ask that the words of Scripture may also be not just signs on a page, but channels of grace into my heart.

—*Origen of Alexandria*

† Read Psalm 46 all the way through several times.

✒ **What stands out to you in this psalm?** Are there any words or phrases that catch your eye? What do you notice about them? Record your thoughts.

_____

_____

_____

_____

_____

_____

_____

_____

_____

_____

_____

_____

_____

† Pray Psalm 46 out loud, as follows.

   O God, come to my assistance; O Lord, make haste to help me!

   Prayerfully read the psalm.

   Glory Be...

TAKE IT WITH YOU:

Copy the part of Psalm 46 that spoke most to you onto a small card or make a note on your smart phone. Carry it with you and meditate on it throughout the week. Repeat it until you know it by heart.

ᒍᕵᏗ WEDNESDAY ᕵᏗᒍ
Reflect

† Find a quiet place where you can read and pray
without distraction.

† Close your eyes and place yourself in God's presence.

† Pray:

*Lord, inspire me to read your Scriptures and to meditate upon them day
and night.... I know that understanding and good intentions are worthless,
unless rooted in your graceful love. I ask that the words of Scripture may
also be not just signs on a page, but channels of grace into my heart.*

—*Origen of Alexandria*

🍂 **Reflect on Psalm 46,** recalling your previous observations.

Continue to read, lingering where your heart draws you. What
do you hear God saying to you, personally? Write down in your
journal the things that come to mind.

_____

† Pray Psalm 46 out loud, as follows.

O God, come to my assistance; O Lord, make haste to help me!

Prayerfully read the psalm.

Glory Be…

✧ THURSDAY ✧
Respond

† Find a quiet place where you can read and pray without distraction.

† Close your eyes and place yourself in God's presence.

† Pray:

Lord, inspire me to read your Scriptures and to meditate upon them day and night.... I know that understanding and good intentions are worthless, unless rooted in your graceful love. I ask that the words of Scripture may also be not just signs on a page, but channels of grace into my heart.

—Origen of Alexandria

† Read Psalm 46 and recall what you have been hearing God say to your heart.

What is your response? Talk to him about it and record your response below.

† Pray Psalm 46 out loud, as follows.

O God, come to my assistance; O Lord, make haste to help me!

Prayerfully read the psalm.

Glory Be…

✍ FRIDAY ✍
Rest

† Find a quiet place where you can read and pray
without distraction.

† Close your eyes and place yourself in God's presence. Pray
Psalm 46 out loud, as follows.

O God, come to my assistance; O Lord, make haste to help me!

Prayerfully read the psalm, recalling the things God has brought
to your mind.

Glory Be…

🐦 **Fix your gaze upon God and rest in his merciful love.**
Allow yourself to be quiet in his presence. Rest as though you are
lying in his arms. Let him fill you with comfort and peace.

Our Father…

> *Peace I leave with you; my peace I give to you; not*
> *as the world gives do I give to you. Let not your*
> *hearts be troubled, neither let them be afraid.*
>
> *—John 14:27*

"He Will Set Me Upon a Rock"
Psalm 61

Assurance of God's Protection

Psalm 61

To the choirmaster: with stringed instruments. A Psalm of David.

1   Hear my cry, O God,
> listen to my prayer;
2   from the end of the earth I call to thee,
> when my heart is faint.
> Lead thou me
> to the rock that is higher than I;
3   for thou art my refuge,
> a strong tower against the enemy.
4   Let me dwell in thy tent for ever!
> Oh to be safe under the shelter of thy wings! *Selah*
5   For thou, O God, hast heard my vows,

thou hast given me the heritage of those who fear
thy name.

6   Prolong the life of the king;

may his years endure to all generations!

7   May he be enthroned for ever before God;

bid steadfast love and faithfulness watch over him!

8   So will I ever sing praises to thy name,

as I pay my vows day after day.

MONDAY
Prepare Your Heart

† Find a quiet place where you can read and pray
without distraction.

† Close your eyes and place yourself in God's presence.

† Read the following:

I have never been fast, and even at four I knew I could never outrun a dog — let alone two big ones, as happened to be the case. They came charging across the lawn and all I could do was cry for help. Richie came out of nowhere and grabbed me, made me stand on his knee and then pushed me up into the tree. I'll never forget the difference it made to be up high, above the danger. The dogs stood with their paws on the trunk, barking and barking and I just sat, secure, in peace.

"Lead me / to the rock that is higher than I," King David wrote in Psalm 61. *"...for you are my refuge, a strong tower against the enemy."*

In the Old Testament, "rock" is a metaphor for God.

To be in the desert where David spent much of his time is to be exposed: to the perils of heat and drought, to boredom, to bandits, to enemies. Shelter is found mainly in rock caves and crevices. Rock is strong and can be relied upon. And on top of a large rock, you can see for miles and ward off enemies. Fortresses are built on high places for a reason.

God is immovable and strong like a rock. He is a safe refuge and fortress. But what if we feel far away from him? How do we get to that rock of safety?

"From the ends of the earth I call to you," David cries, *"when my heart is faint…*

"Lead me
    to the rock that is higher than I."

The lines are broken up like that in my Bible, with "Lead me" set off by itself. It stands out and begs for attention. This is a psalm for people who are far from God, who need help getting to the rock like I needed help getting into that tree. But it's not a cry of desperation. It's full of assurance that God will reach down and take David where he needs to be, to be safe.

David asks God to lead him to safety based on the fact that God has done so in the past: he's been his refuge, a strong tower, a God who has "given me the heritage of those who fear thy name." God promised Israel the heritage of the Promised Land, and he gave it to David and his successors forever. David *knew* God's promises and his faithfulness to his people. It was because of God's character and past actions that David had faith to rely on God's help in his present situation.

We have the same reasons to trust. God is the same yesterday, today, and forever. Make this psalm yours! At the end of it, David determines to sing praises and pay his vows "day after day." We can do that too: put one foot in front of the other, daily calling on the Lord in prayer and praising him. With that movement, we stretch our arms to God and beg to be held within his stronger arms, "safe within the shelter of (his) wings" (vs. 4).

As you meditate on Psalm 61 this week, recall that the Church fathers saw the "shadow of God's wings" as the shadow of the Cross. Jesus's arms are outstretched even now, reaching out and calling us to himself.

† Pray Psalm 61 out loud, as follows.

O God, come to my assistance; O Lord, make haste to help me!

Prayerfully read the psalm.

Glory Be…

TUESDAY
Read

† Find a quiet place where you can read and pray without distraction.

† Close your eyes and place yourself in God's presence.

† Pray:

Lord, inspire me to read your Scriptures and to meditate upon them day and night…. I know that understanding and good intentions are worthless, unless rooted in your graceful love. I ask that the words of Scripture may also be not just signs on a page, but channels of grace into my heart.

——*Origen of Alexandria*

† Read Psalm 61 all the way through several times.

What stands out to you in this psalm? Are there any words or phrases that catch your eye? What do you notice about them Record your thoughts.

_____

_____

_____

_____

_____

_____

_____

_____

_____

_____

_____

_____

_____

_____

† Pray Psalm 61 out loud, as follows.

O God, come to my assistance; O Lord, make haste to help me!

Prayerfully read the psalm.

Glory Be…

TAKE IT WITH YOU:

Copy the part of Psalm 61 that spoke most to you onto a small card or make a note on your smart phone. Carry it with you and meditate on it throughout the week. Repeat it until you know it by heart.

WEDNESDAY
Reflect

† Find a quiet place where you can read and pray without distraction.

† Close your eyes and place yourself in God's presence.

† Pray:

Lord, inspire me to read your Scriptures and to meditate upon them day and night.... I know that understanding and good intentions are worthless, unless rooted in your graceful love. I ask that the words of Scripture may also be not just signs on a page, but channels of grace into my heart.

—*Origen of Alexandria*

Reflect on Psalm 61, recalling your previous observations. Continue to read, lingering where your heart draws you. What do you hear God saying to you, personally? Write down in your journal the things that come to mind.

_____

_____

_____

_____

_____

_____

_____

_____

† Pray Psalm 61 out loud, as follows.

O God, come to my assistance; O Lord, make haste to help me!

Prayerfully read the psalm.

Glory Be…

THURSDAY
Respond

† Find a quiet place where you can read and pray without distraction.

† Close your eyes and place yourself in God's presence.

† Pray:

Lord, inspire me to read your Scriptures and to meditate upon them day and night…. I know that understanding and good intentions are worthless, unless rooted in your graceful love. I ask that the words of Scripture may also be not just signs on a page, but channels of grace into my heart.

——*Origen of Alexandria*

† Read Psalm 61 and recall what you have been hearing God say to your heart.

What is your response? Talk to him about it. Record your response below.

_____

_____

_____

_____

_____

_____

_____

_____

_____

_____

_____

_____

_____

_____

_____

_____

_____

_____

_____

_____

_____

_____

_____

_____

_____

† Pray Psalm 61 out loud, as follows.

O God, come to my assistance; O Lord, make haste to help me!

Prayerfully read the psalm.

Glory Be...

FRIDAY
Rest

† Find a quiet place where you can read and pray without distraction.

† Close your eyes and place yourself in God's presence. Pray Psalm 61 out loud, as follows.

O God, come to my assistance; O Lord, make haste to help me!

Prayerfully read the psalm, recalling the things God has brought to your mind.

Glory Be...

Fix your gaze upon God and rest in his merciful love. Allow yourself to be quiet in his presence. Rest as though you are lying in his arms. Let him fill you with comfort and peace.

Our Father...

The eternal God is your dwelling place, and underneath are the everlasting arms.

—Deut 33:27

He Leads Me Beside Still Waters
Psalm 23

The Divine Shepherd

Psalm 23

A Psalm of David.

1   The Lord is my shepherd, I shall not want;

2   he makes me lie down in green pastures.

> He leads me beside still waters[1];

3   he restores my soul[2].

> He leads me in paths of righteousness[3]
> for his name's sake.

4   Even though I walk through the valley of the shadow of death[4],

> I fear no evil;

> for thou art with me;

---

1   Heb *the waters of rest*
2   Or *life*
3   Or *right paths*
4   Or *the valley of deep darkness*

thy rod and thy staff,

they comfort me.

5 Thou preparest a table before me

in the presence of my enemies;

thou anointest my head with oil,

my cup overflows.

6 Surely[5] goodness and mercy[6] shall follow me

all the days of my life;

and I shall dwell in the house of the Lord

for ever.[7]

---

5 Or *Only*
6 Or *kindness*
7 Or *as long as I live*

MONDAY
Prepare Your Heart

Our final psalm is not one that calls for God to help, but one that assures us of his loving care, however far away he might seem at times.

† Find a quiet place where you can read and pray without distraction.

† Close your eyes and place yourself in God's presence.

† Read the following:

"By Still Waters" was Mother's name for our house. I never gave it much thought, beyond that it had a nice ring to it. But sitting by the still waters of a mountain lake and soaking in the quiet, I thank her for instilling in me the knowledge of the possibility of peace:

She named her house "By Still Waters" not because life was smooth but because the world is a battleground. And she knew that in God there is peace that can't come from the world.

She named the house "By Still Waters" because God gave our family peace even in sickness and hardship and chaos. She longed to provide a place of peace for others who were war-torn and weary. If that meant bringing refugees and wounded souls into our home, so be it. We would pour ourselves out for them, surround them with prayer and love, and send them forth in God's peace.

Even before we could read, my brothers and I memorized Psalm 23. We would recite the whole thing together, sometimes, at the dinner table. We even sang the last verse, over and over. I sing it today when I need reassurance.

The world is full of unrest and it's starting to hit close to home. Sometimes I am afraid. I send waves of worry into my life as though that will repel whatever is out there, as though that will keep evil at bay.

It won't, of course. But sooner or later, *"Yea, though I walk through the valley of the shadow of death, I will fear no evil[8]"* wells up within me. Thank you, Mom and Dad, for making us memorize! That inner voice continues: *"For thou art with me."* *"He maketh me to lie down in green pastures: he leadeth me beside the still waters. He restoreth my soul."*

Looking out over the lake, I can bask in the quiet and beauty. But when my world is noisy or falling apart — God, I am grateful for the peace that you pour through my soul!

 † Pray Psalm 23 out loud, as follows.

 O God, come to my assistance; O Lord, make haste to help me!

 Prayerfully read the psalm.

 Glory Be…

---

8   I learned Psalm 23 in the King James Version.

⤳ TUESDAY ⤲
Read

† Find a quiet place where you can read and pray
   without distraction.

† Close your eyes and place yourself in God's presence.

† Pray:

*Lord, inspire me to read your Scriptures and to meditate upon them day
and night.... I know that understanding and good intentions are worthless,
unless rooted in your graceful love. I ask that the words of Scripture may
also be not just signs on a page, but channels of grace into my heart.*

—*Origen of Alexandria*

† Read Psalm 23 all the way through several times.

What stands out to you in this psalm? Are there any
words or phrases that catch your eye? What do you notice about
them? Record your thought.

_____

_____

_____

_____

_____

_____

_____

_____

† Pray Psalm 23 out loud, as follows.

O God, come to my assistance; O Lord, make haste to help me!

Prayerfully read the psalm.

Glory Be…

TAKE IT WITH YOU:

Copy the part of Psalm 23 that spoke most to you onto a small card or make a note on your smart phone. Carry it with you and meditate on it throughout the week. Repeat it until you know it by heart.

⁓ WEDNESDAY ⁓
Reflect

† Find a quiet place where you can read and pray without distraction.

† Close your eyes and place yourself in God's presence.

† Pray:

Lord, inspire me to read your Scriptures and to meditate upon them day and night.... I know that understanding and good intentions are worthless, unless rooted in your graceful love. I ask that the words of Scripture may also be not just signs on a page, but channels of grace into my heart.

—*Origen of Alexandria*

Reflect on Psalm 23, recalling your previous observations.

Continue to read, lingering where your heart draws you. What do you hear God saying to you, personally? Write down in your journal the things that come to mind.

_____

_____

_____

_____

_____

_____

_____

_____

_____

_____

_____

_____

_____

_____

_____

_____

_____

_____

† Pray Psalm 23 out loud, as follows.

O God, come to my assistance; O Lord, make haste to help me!

Prayerfully read the psalm.

Glory Be…

✐ THURSDAY ✐
Respond

† Find a quiet place where you can read and pray
without distraction.

† Close your eyes and place yourself in God's presence.

† Pray:

*Lord, inspire me to read your Scriptures and to meditate upon them day
and night.... I know that understanding and good intentions are worthless,
unless rooted in your graceful love. I ask that the words of Scripture may
also be not just signs on a page, but channels of grace into my heart.*

—Origen of Alexandria

† Read Psalm 23 and recall what you have been hearing God
say to your heart.

What is your response? Talk to him about it. Record your
response below.

_____

_____

_____

_____

_____

_____

_____

† Pray Psalm 23 out loud, as follows.

O God, come to my assistance; O Lord, make haste to help me!

Prayerfully read the psalm.

Glory Be…

⌒ FRIDAY ⌒
Rest

† Find a quiet place where you can read and pray
without distraction.

† Close your eyes and place yourself in God's presence. Pray
Psalm 23 out loud, as follows.

O God, come to my assistance; O Lord, make haste to help me!

Prayerfully read the psalm, recalling the things God has brought
to your mind.

Glory Be…

🦢 Fix your gaze upon God and rest in his merciful love. Allow
yourself to be quiet in his presence. Rest as though you are lying
in his arms. Let him fill you with comfort and peace.

Our Father…

> *Have no anxiety about anything, but in everything*
> *by prayer and supplication with thanksgiving let your*
> *requests be made known to God. And the peace*
> *of God, which passes all understanding, will keep*
> *your hearts and your minds in Christ Jesus.*
>
> *—Philippians 4:6-7*

> *I am the good shepherd.*
>
> *—Jesus (John 10:14)*

Continuing in the Word

"Exercise your mind, feed it daily with Holy Scripture"

—*St. Jerome*

I hope you've been blessed by your daily journey through these psalms. Now, consider setting aside a regular time each day to continue connecting with God in his Word and growing in your relationship with the Lord.

Here are seven ideas to get you started:

1. **Get a lectionary** and read the Gospel every day for a year (don't wait to go to Mass). You can also find the readings on an easy-to-use calendar at http://www.usccb.org/

2. **Read a Psalm a day** until you've read all 150. When you're done, go back to your favorites. Or get familiar with praying the Liturgy of the Hours.

3. **Read through the New Testament.** Take your time, even if it's just a few verses or chapters a day. Let it soak in. Listen and pray to meet the Word in his words.

4. I once spent an entire school year reading **a chapter of Proverbs a day**. There are 31 chapters, so it's easy to go to the day you're on.

5. Don't be afraid to **read something good over and over.** You might even memorize a book that way, without trying. Think what God could do in your soul if his Word begins to be part of you....

6. **Read the entire story of salvation** with the 90-day *Bible Timeline* reading plan from The Great Adventure Catholic Bible Study Program. It'll take you from Creation to the Church (fourteen books in all) in just three months. Download a checklist at **http://bit.ly/1QcATn1** or read with the help of the *Bible Timeline Guided Journal*, available from Ascension Press.

7. **Read through those same readings at a slower pace**, in one year instead of over three months, by reading just one chapter a day.

Let me know what you plan and how you get on with it! You can email me at sarah@ComeIntotheWord.com. And may the Lord richly bless you as you read.

Visit www.ComeIntotheWord.com for weekly reflections on the Bible and the Catholic faith and helpful information on reading and studying the Bible.

Sarah Christmyer is co-developer and founding editor of *The Great Adventure* Catholic Bible study program. The author of numerous Bible studies, she speaks at conferences and retreats on topics related to Scripture and the Catholic faith. Sarah is an adjunct faculty member at St. Charles Borromeo Seminary, Philadelphia. She blogs at her website — www.ComeIntotheWord.com — and at www.BibleStudyforCatholics.com and www.CatholicVineyard.com.

87550210R00071

Made in the USA
Columbia, SC
20 January 2018